Drama for Students, Volume 29

Project Editor: Sara Constantakis Rights Acquisition and Management: Leitha Etheridge-Sims, Tracie Richardson Composition: Evi Abou-El-Seoud Manufacturing: Rhonda Dover

Imaging: John Watkins

Product Design: Pamela A. E. Galbreath, Jennifer Wahi Content Conversion: Katrina Coach Product Manager: Meggin Condino © 2012 Gale, Cengage Learning

ALL RIGHTS RESERVED. No part of this work covered by the copyright herein may be reproduced, transmitted, stored, or used in any form or by any means graphic, electronic, or mechanical, including but not limited to photocopying, recording, scanning, digitizing, taping, Web distribution, information networks, or information storage and retrieval systems, except as permitted under Section 107 or 108 of the 1976 United States Copyright Act, without the prior written permission of the publisher.

Since this page cannot legibly accommodate all copyright notices, the acknowledgments constitute an extension of the copyright notice.

For product information and technology assistance, contact us at **Gale Customer Support, 1-800-877-4253**.

For permission to use material from this text or product, submit all requests online at www.cengage.com/permissions.

Further permissions questions can be emailed to **permissionrequest@cengage.com** While every effort has been made to ensure the reliability of the information presented in this publication, Gale, a part of Cengage Learning, does not guarantee the accuracy of the data contained herein. Gale accepts no payment for listing; and inclusion in the publication of any organization, agency, institution, publication, service, or individual does not imply endorsement of the editors or publisher. Errors brought to the attention of the publisher and verified to the satisfaction of the publisher will be corrected in future editions.

Gale
27500 Drake Rd.
Farmington Hills, MI, 48331-3535

ISBN-13: 978-0-7876-8125-8
ISBN-10: 0-7876-8125-3
ISSN 1094-9232

This title is also available as an e-book.

ISBN-13: 978-1-4144-4941-8
ISBN-10: 1-4144-4941-0
Contact your Gale, a part of Cengage Learning sales representative for ordering information.

Printed in Mexico
1 2 3 4 5 6 7 16 15 14 13 12

Guys and Dolls

Jo Swerling, Abe Burrows and Frank Loesser

1950

Introduction

Guys and Dolls is a work of musical theater that premiered in 1950. Inspired by short stories by Damon Runyon that were published in 1932 under the same title, *Guys and Dolls* was adapted for the stage by Jo Swerling and Abe Burrows. Frank Loesser wrote the music and lyrics.

Set in New York City, the play does not

specify its time frame, but references in the story suggest that the play's writers updated the setting to make the play contemporary with its 1950 production. The story explores the world of illegal gambling and betting, and its action is generated by a bet between Nathan Detroit, who is seeking a location for an illegal dice game but needs money to pay a bribe, and Sky Masterson, a worldly and wealthy gambler known for taking on bizarre bets. Nathan bets Sky that Sky cannot get Sarah, the prim and devout Christian of the Save-a-Soul Mission, to go to Havana, Cuba, with him. Sky takes the bet, setting off a chain of events that leads through improbable maneuvering to a happy ending. Throughout the play, the notion of romantic love is at once the source of derision and the butt of jokes but also an ideal for which the main characters all strive.

The Guys and Dolls Book, which contains the full text of the play as well as the lyrics to all of the songs, was published in 1982. The play won five Tony Awards in 1951, including Best Musical.

Author Biography

Abe Burrows

Burrows adapted Swerling's draft of the script for the theatrical version of *Guys and Dolls* around Loesser's songs, and he is credited with writing the bulk of the playbook. Burrows was born on December 18, 1910, in New York. After writing for radio and television, he began writing for the stage in his debut effort, *Guys and Dolls*, revising and completing the script begun by Jo Swerling. Following the successful run of *Guys and Dolls*, Burrows continued to work as both a playwright and director, writing and directing his first post–*Guys and Dolls* effort, *Can-Can*, in 1954. By the mid-1960s, Burrows focused on directing. Burrows died of pneumonia on May 17, 1985.

Frank Loesser

Loesser wrote the music and lyrics to *Guys and Dolls*. According to Caryl Brahms and Ned Sherrin, who wrote a biographical essay on Loesser for *The Guys and Dolls Book*, "It was Loesser who threw out Swerling's original book, but perversely he still wrote his score around it."

Loesser was born on June 29, 1910, in New York. In the early portion of his career, Loesser wrote lyrics and sketches for both radio and live vaudeville productions. He collaborated with a number of other songwriters for screen and stage. Loesser wrote the music and lyrics for *Guys and Dolls*, working with Burrows, who wrote the final version of the playbook begun by Swerling. Loesser also worked on the 1955 film adaptation of *Guys and Dolls*, composing several new numbers for this production. Loesser continued to compose for both film and theater, writing the music and lyrics for the 1961 Broadway production *How to Succeed in Business Without Really Trying*, another award-winning play. It won the 1962 Tony Award for Best Musical, along with the Pulitzer Prize for Drama. Loesser died of lung cancer on July 26, 1969.

Jo Swerling

Swerling was originally hired to write the playbook for *Guys and Dolls*, but he was replaced by Burrows, who revised and built upon what Swerling had begun.

Swerling was born on April 8, 1897, in Baridchov, Russia. As a child, he and his family escaped the czarist regime and landed in New York. Swerling moved to Chicago and secured a position with the *Chicago Herald and Examiner* newspaper. He began writing for the theater after writing a review for the Marx Brothers' vaudeville act. His early plays include *One of Us* (1918) and *Kibitzer* (1929). The success of his plays encouraged him to pursue a career in screenwriting, and he wrote a number of films in the 1930s and 1940s. In 1950,

Swerling began a playbook inspired by characters and stories in Damon Runyon's 1932 collection *Guys and Dolls*. Burrows completed the playbook Swerling began, but Swerling is still credited for his early work on the play. Swerling died in 1964.

Plot Summary

Act 1, Scene 1

Guys and Dolls is divided into two acts. The first act opens with a musical number, "Runyonland," playing as various individuals make their way across the stage, which is set as Broadway, the famous street in the theater district of New York City. The stage directions refer to "bobby soxers" crossing the stage. The use of this term suggests that the time frame in which the play is set is contemporary with its production in 1950. The term refers to teenage girls of the 1940s and 1950s who dressed in skirts paired with a short cuffed style of sock known as bobby socks. Other figures moving across the stage include police officers, chorus girls from a Broadway show, prostitutes, an elderly female street vendor, a boxer and his manager, an actress, and sightseers. Benny Southstreet enters reading a racing form and is shortly joined by Nicely-Nicely Johnson and Rusty Charlie, all gamblers. The three sing a number about horse racing and betting, "Fugue for Tinhorns." This number is shortly followed by the entrance of Sarah and the Mission Band, who sing "Follow the Fold." Sarah then preaches to the people still gathered on the street, including the gamblers, to repent. Everyone ignores her or walks away, and Sarah and the other missionaries leave, dejected. Her good looks are noticed by Nicely and

Benny. Another gambler, Harry the Horse, enters, and the men discuss the difficulties that Nathan Detroit is having in finding a place to hold a crap game. (Craps is a dice game in which bets are placed on the outcome of a player's roll.)

Media Adaptations

- In 1955, Swerling, Burrows, and Loesser's stage musical *Guys and Dolls* was adapted for the big screen. The film adaptation was written and directed by Joseph L. Mankiewicz and starred Frank Sinatra as Nathan, Vivian Blaine as Adelaide, Marlon Brando as Sky, and Jean Simmons as Sarah. The film was released on DVD in 2006 by MGM Studios.

- The original cast recording of the songs from the 1950 musical version is available as an MP3 download.

The album was released in 1992 by RCA Victor.
- The cast recording from the 1992 Broadway revival of *Guys and Dolls* starring Nathan Lane is available as a CD and MP3 download; it was released in 2009 by Masterworks Broadway.

Lieutenant Brannigan is trying to find and arrest gamblers, and he has reminded business owners that it is illegal to allow their premises to be used for gambling. Nathan enters, looking depressed, and after Brannigan's departure reveals to his friends that he has found a place to host the high-stakes crap game, but the owner of Biltmore Garage, Joey Biltmore, wants one thousand dollars in payment, which Nathan does not have. A number of other crap shooters enter gradually, and together they sing about Nathan's unfailing ability to find a place for "the oldest established permanent floating crap game in New York," in the musical number "The Oldest Established." One of the dice players informs Nathan that Sky Masterson is in town; his reputation as a high-stakes player is discussed.

Adelaide arrives on the scene, and she and Nathan discuss their fourteen-year anniversary of being engaged. Nathan rushes her off as she begins to talk about marriage, and Sky arrives. Sky observes, when Adelaide's name comes up, that Nathan is "trapped." He advocates a freer lifestyle and assures Nathan that he could take any woman he wanted with him to Havana. As the Save-a-Soul Mission Band, led by Sarah, reappears, Nathan seizes an opportunity for a bet he believes he cannot lose: he bets Sky that he cannot get Sarah to go with him to Havana.

Act 1, Scene 2

At the Save-a-Soul Mission, Sarah Brown and Arvide Abernathy, who is Sarah's grandfather and who also works for the Save-a-Soul Mission, discuss the apparent futility of trying to get sinners to repent in this part of town. Sky enters the mission and begins to try and convince them that he would like to give up gambling. Arvide leaves the two of them to talk. Sky flirts with Sarah, assuring her that he is such a sinner he will need private instructions to overcome his ways. Aware that the mission has not been successful in bringing in sinners, he promises Sarah that he will fill the place with sinners if she only has dinner with him—in Havana. In the number "I'll Know," Sarah sings about what her true love will be like. Sky joins in, after chastising Sarah on her unwillingness to take chances, and describes the chemistry he will feel with his true love when he meets her. He then kisses Sarah. The stage directions indicate that Sarah looks entranced and moved by what has happened but nevertheless "belts him one across the chops."

Act 1, Scene 3

In this brief scene, Nathan is talking on the phone to Joey Biltmore, the owner of the Biltmore Garage, where Nathan would like to host the next crap game. Joey insists on receiving one thousand dollars up front.

Act 1, Scene 4

This scene opens at the Hot Box, the nightclub where Adelaide sings and dances with the Hot Box girls. After Adelaide performs the number "Bushel and a Peck," she sits with Nathan, who has come to see her, and tells him of her impending raise, such that now they can get married. She also informs him of the elaborate fiction she has conveyed to her mother: she married Nathan long ago and they now have five children. Another dancer, Mimi, enters, looking for an earring. Seeing Nathan, she angrily reproaches him because her boyfriend, Society Max, has broken a date with her to attend Nathan's dice game. After Mimi leaves, Nathan hurriedly reassures Adelaide that they will get married; he then rushes off. Adelaide, who has been fighting a cold since the play began, reads from a book the doctor has given her, alternating between speaking and singing in the number "Adelaide's Lament." She discovers that her symptoms may have developed as a result of the emotional struggle she endures owing to Nathan's failure to marry her.

Act 1, Scene 5

On a street off Broadway, Nicely and Benny

discuss the way women unnecessarily distract men. Nicely has just observed Sky following Sarah and the Mission Band when Benny comments that Nathan is probably trying to see Adelaide, as she is angry with him again. The two sing the number "Guys and Dolls" and observe the way men behave irrationally or outlandishly in their pursuit of women.

Act 1, Scene 6

Back at the mission, Sarah and Arvide are approached by General Cartwright, a mission administrator. She informs them that the mission will have to close. Sky, who has wandered by, overhears the conversation and persuades General Cartwright to wait until after the next meeting to make her decision. Sarah personally guarantees the presence of a dozen sinners at the next meeting.

Act 1, Scene 7

On a street off Broadway, Benny and Harry the Horse are ready for the crap game, but Nathan has still not received the money he thought Sky would have delivered by now. Consequently, he has not been able to pay Joey Biltmore for the use of the Biltmore Garage. Another high-stakes gambler, Big Jule, has also arrived, and he threatens Nathan, who tries to placate him with promises that he will still find a place for the dice game. Lieutenant Brannigan approaches, suspicious of the men. As he begins to question them, Adelaide appears, and

Benny attempts to deter Brannigan by telling him that everyone is gathered for Nathan's bachelor dinner, as he is about to marry Adelaide. Nathan tries to dampen Adelaide's eagerness by informing her that they still need to get a license and blood test, but he is dismayed to hear Brannigan suggest they drive upstate to Buffalo, New York, where they would not need a blood test, and elope.

Act 1, Scene 8

The scene opens in a café in Havana, Cuba, where Sarah is ordering a ham sandwich. The stage directions indicate a quick change in the scenery to indicate that Sky and Sarah are now sightseeing. They sit down at a street café where Sky orders Sarah a drink that she thinks is a type of milk shake but is really a rum-based cocktail. She innocently gulps down two. After another quick scene change, Sky and Sarah are seen entering another bar, where Sarah orders two more "dulce de leche" drinks. A female Cuban dancer begins to flirt with Sky, and a male Cuban dancer flirts with Sarah, until a fight breaks out with some of the other Cubans at the bar. Sarah smashes a bottle on someone's head before Sky forcibly drags her out.

Act 1, Scene 9

In the street outside the bar, Sky asks Sarah how she is feeling. She replies by singing the number, "If I Were a Bell," demonstrating her inebriation and elation. Sky begins to feel guilty and confesses that he brought her to Havana on a bet. Sarah does not seem to care. Although Sarah expresses a wish to stay in Havana, Sky picks her up and exits, heading for their plane.

Act 1, Scene 10

Sarah and Sky are standing outside the mission at four in the morning. Sarah thanks Sky for returning her safely. Adelaide enters, and after Sky introduces Sarah and Adelaide, Adelaide explains that her friends have just given her a wedding shower and that she and Nathan are eloping the next night. Sky sings the number "My Time of Day," confiding to Sarah that this predawn hour is his favorite, and she is the only one with whom he would want to share it. He also tells her that his real name is Obediah; she is the first person he has ever told this. He then sings "I've Never Been in Love Before," and she joins in. They then kiss, but they are soon interrupted by the arrival of Arvide and the Mission Band, who have been out all night. Suddenly, as Sky opens the door, Benny, Nicely, and Nathan hurry out of the mission. Other gamblers emerge as well, and everyone rushes away, but Sky grabs Nathan, who explains that they were gambling. Big Jule yells angrily after Nathan that he is losing ten thousand dollars. Brannigan arrives with two other officers and informs Sarah that the mission was being used for Nathan's floating crap game. Sarah is shocked, and Sky explains to her that he knew nothing of Nathan's plans for the mission. When Sky asks when he will see her again, Sarah tells him they are through.

Act 2, Scene 1

The second act opens at the Hot Box, where Adelaide and the Hot Box Girls sing the number "Take Back Your Mink." Sky and Nicely are in the audience, and Nicely asks Sky to tell Adelaide that Nathan had to go to Pittsburgh to help a sick aunt, an obvious lie. Nicely tells Sky the game is still going on, and Sky wants the location. Nicely shouts a botched version of Nathan's message to Adelaide before he leaves. Adelaide rushes over to Sky, expressing her dismay, telling Sky that Nathan promised to change. Sky admonishes her for wanting to change Nathan, and Adelaide scolds him and men like him who refuse to settle down like other people. Sky asks her why she does not just find another man, and Adelaide explains that she loves Nathan; when Sky falls in love someday, she says, he will understand. Sky exits, and Adelaide sings "Adelaide's Second Lament," a reprised (repeated, sometimes with variations) version of her earlier song.

Act 2, Scene 2

On 48th Street, Sarah and Arvide discuss what happened with the gamblers using the mission. Arvide attempts to assure Sarah that they can still help such people and points out that even a man like Sky Masterson came to the mission seeking refuge. Sarah counters that Sky came to the mission seeking her. Arvide says that he knew Sky had his eye on Sarah, but he did not anticipate her falling for Sky. Sarah assures him she will get over Sky, but Arvide asks her why she would want to. Arvide sings the number "More I Cannot Wish You," insisting that all he wants for her is to find love. Sky arrives and confesses that the gamblers—the sinners to be saved, showing the necessity of keeping the mission open—will not be at the mission after all. Seeing that Sarah is angry with him, Sky insists he will still try and convince twelve sinners to be at the mission for the meeting that night. Sarah dismisses him, but Arvide threatens to expose Sky as a man who does not honor his bets if he does not deliver the men he promised.

Act 2, Scene 3

The scene opens in the sewer, where the crap game continues. Many of the men are getting ready to depart, but Big Jule wants to keep playing. In Nathan's conversation with Big Jule, Nathan implies that Big Jule, who will use only his own dice, is not playing fairly. After directly accusing Big Jule of cheating, Nathan is warned by Harry about what Big Jule could do to him. Nathan assures him that even death would be welcome at this point, since he has lost all his money, after risking so much to put the game together and even promising to get married in order to arrange the game.

Sky and Nicely arrive. When Big Jule threatens to prevent Sky from talking to the other men, Sky punches him and takes his gun away. Sky asks the men to come to the mission, but they scoff. As he turns to leave, Nathan apologizes for not yet having the money to pay him for losing the bet on Sarah. Instead, Sky pays Nathan, telling him that Nathan won the bet after all. Again, Sky turns to leave, and Nathan tells Big Jule that he now has enough money to play him—but they will use Sky's dice this time. Harry tells Nathan that without using his own (loaded) dice, Big Jule cannot make a winning roll "to save his soul." This gives Sky an idea: he tells the men he will roll them for their souls, that is, if he wins, they come with him to the mission; if he loses, he pays them each one thousand dollars. Sky sings "Luck Be a Lady Tonight," and the other men join in, each hoping for luck to be with him in the dice game to follow.

Act 2, Scene 4

The crap shooters are all making their way through the streets when Nathan runs into Adelaide. Despite her initial indignation with him, Adelaide warms up and shortly persuades him to still elope. However, when Nathan sees Benny and Nicely, he realizes he must go to the mission. Adelaide does not believe him when he tells her he is going to a prayer meeting. The two sing a duet, "Sue Me," in which Nathan pleads for her understanding and Adelaide accuses him of making false promises.

Act 2, Scene 5

Inside the mission, Sarah, Arvide, and the Mission Band members are gathered, and General Cartwright begins to wonder whether the promised sinners will appear. Moments later, Sky arrives with the gamblers. When the men are called upon to confess their sins, Harry the Horse reveals that they are only at the mission because Sky beat them in a dice game. Sarah is dismayed as she makes the matter clear to General Cartwright, but the general is pleased, feeling as though having gotten the sinners to the mission in this fashion is a great accomplishment. The men continue to testify to their sinful natures. Brannigan appears, but he is hushed by Nathan and made to sit and join the group. When it is Nicely's turn, he sings the number "Sit Down, You're Rockin' the Boat." The other men join in. At the end of the number, Brannigan reveals that he is there to arrest the men for gambling in the mission the previous night. He asks Sarah whether she can identify the men, but she replies that she has never seen them before. Frustrated, Brannigan leaves. Nathan confesses to the missionaries that he and the other men did gamble at the mission and that they are all sorry. He then apologizes to Sarah for making the bet with Sky about being able to take her to Havana.

Act 2, Scene 6

Adelaide and Sarah run into each other near Times Square. They talk about the ways they wish Sky and Nathan were different and how they wish they could change them. Sarah reveals that Nathan was at the prayer meeting at the mission, so Adelaide finds out that this time Nathan has not actually lied to her. Adelaide and Sarah realize that they have been approaching the matter the wrong way. In the number "Marry the Man Today," they discuss a new philosophy: marry the man today, and change him afterward.

Act 2, Scene 7

On Broadway, many of the same people who bustled across the stage when the play opened are present once again. Adelaide, dressed in a wedding gown, arrives at a newsstand looking for Nathan. Brannigan is buying a paper. Nathan appears from behind the newsstand, and when he pulls down the shade on the stand, it reads "Nathan Detroit's News Stand." He emerges dressed for his wedding, but he soon frets that he has not found a place for it to take place. The Mission Band enters, and Sky is now dressed in one of the mission's uniforms as well. Nathan asks Sky if he and Adelaide can get married at the mission, but Arvide replies instead. Arvide recently performed the marriage ceremony for Sky and Sarah at the mission; he would be happy to perform the ceremony for Nathan and Adelaide as well. The play closes with a reprise of the "Guys and Dolls" number.

Characters

Arvide Abernathy

Arvide is Sarah's grandfather. Like Sarah, he works at the Save-a-Soul Mission. He encourages Sarah when she despairs that the mission is not having a positive effect on the sinners in the area. Realizing Sarah is in love with Sky, he suggests that she overlook the fact that Sky is a gambler and encourages her to follow her heart.

Adelaide

Adelaide is Nathan Detroit's fiancée. A performer at the Hot Box, Adelaide has been engaged to Nathan for fourteen years, and she has created an elaborate fiction of their life together for her mother, to whom she has written about a wedding that never happened and children that do not exist. She repeatedly pleads with Nathan to marry her and give up gambling, and she takes him back every time he apologizes for lying to her. Throughout the play, she has a cold that, after consulting a medical book, she attributes to the fact that she loves a man who will not marry her. She and Sarah resolve to forget about changing their men until after they marry them.

Agatha

Agatha is a member of the Mission Band.

Angie the Ox

Angie the Ox is one of the crap shooters.

Brandy Bottle Bates

Brandy Bottle Bates is one of the crap shooters.

Joey Biltmore

Joey Biltmore does not appear on stage; only his voice is heard. Joey talks to Nathan on the phone, insisting that Nathan may only use the Biltmore Garage for the crap game if Nathan pays him one thousand dollars first.

Lieutenant Brannigan

Brannigan is a police officer who attempts to shut down the illegal gambling ring run by Nathan. Although he succeeds in making it difficult for Nathan to set up a game, he is unable to prosecute any gamblers during the course of the play.

Sergeant Sarah Brown

Sarah is a missionary who is focused on compelling the sinners of New York City to repent their sins and renew their faith at the Save-a-Soul Mission where she works. Despite her prim demeanor, she longs for love. Sky Masterson believes that her notion of love is one that few men could live up to. Sky propositions Sarah, promising her sinners to fill up the mission if she will accompany him to Havana. She initially refuses. After Sky kisses Sarah, she slaps him, but she eventually agrees to accompany him on the condition that he can actually bring in a dozen sinners to the mission; she needs to prove to her superiors that the mission is necessary and should not be closed. In Havana, Sarah unwittingly drinks alcohol, becomes tipsy, and begins to open up to the possibility of a romance with Sky. When the two return to New York, they profess their love for one another. Sarah, however, comes to the realization that she and Sky are too different to be a suitable match. He nonetheless delivers on his promise to bring the sinners to the mission, thereby saving it from being closed. Sarah resolves to pursue her relationship with Sky, and they marry at the end of the play.

Calvin

Calvin is a member of the Mission Band.

General Cartwright

General Cartwright is an administrator for the mission. She tells Arvide and Sarah and the others that the mission will be closing. Sky persuades her to wait until after the next meeting (to which he has promised Sarah he will bring a dozen sinners) to make her decision.

Rusty Charley

Rusty Charley is a gambler who appears in the first scene, singing with Benny and Nicely.

Nathan Detroit

Nathan is a gambler. He runs a floating crap game, that is, a game that moves from location to location to protect the gamblers from being discovered by the police. Nathan repeatedly professes his love for Adelaide, but he is obviously reluctant to commit to marriage, given that the couple's engagement has lasted fourteen years. Much of the play's action is generated by a bet Nathan makes with Sky. Seeking a location for the dice game, Nathan needs money to pay Joey Biltmore for the use of his garage. Consequently, Nathan bets Sky that Sky cannot get Sarah to go to Havana with him. Sky's pursuit of Sarah parallels Nathan's pursuit of a location for his crap game. After the prayer meeting at the mission—a meeting that Nathan, along with the other gamblers, is forced to attend after losing a bet to Sky—Nathan appears to seek a respectable way of living. He buys a newsstand and is finally prepared to marry Adelaide.

Harry the Horse

Harry the Horse, another gambler, arrives in

New York with Big Jule and serves as one of his underlings.

Hot Horse Herbie

Hot Horse Herbie is one of the crap shooters.

Hot Box Girls

The Hot Box Girls are Adelaide's fellow performers at the nightclub, the Hot Box. They throw her a bridal shower when it appears as though Nathan and Adelaide are going to elope.

Nicely-Nicely Johnson

Nicely is one of Nathan's friends and fellow gamblers. With Benny Southstreet, Nicely attempts to help Nathan as much as possible, by running errands and delivering messages for him or helping to keep Adelaide at bay. Nicely and Benny both feel that Adelaide is a distraction for Nathan.

Big Jule

Big Jule is a high-stakes gambler from Chicago. He threatens Nathan with physical violence if Nathan cannot find a place for a game of craps. During the game, Big Jule cheats, leaves everyone broke, and threatens Nathan when Nathan stands up to him. Like the other gamblers, he loses his game with Sky and must report to the prayer meeting at the mission.

Liverlips Louis

Liverlips Louis is one of the crap shooters.

Martha

Martha is a member of the Mission Band.

Sky Masterson

Sky Masterson is a high-stakes gambler. Depicted as cool-headed and suave, Sky is known for taking on strange bets. He is wise to Nathan's attempt to trick him into taking a rigged bet regarding the number of desserts sold at a local café. He accepts Nathan's bet that he cannot take any woman he chooses with him to Havana;

Nathan selects Sarah. Sky initially pursues Sarah only to win the bet, but he has fallen in love with her by the time they return from Havana. He persuades her to go by promising her a mission full of sinners, and Sarah agrees to the Havana trip only to keep the mission open. Although Sky is disheartened by Sarah's decision to stop seeing him after the gamblers are discovered at the mission, Sky follows through on his promise: after winning a series of dice rolls, he delivers the gamblers to the mission. Because his efforts are successful, General Cartwright decides that the mission may remain operational. When Nathan and Adelaide are looking for a place to have their wedding, Arvide informs them that he has recently performed the wedding of Sky and Sarah at the mission. Sky is seen at the play's end working as a missionary, dressed in uniform and preaching to people on the street about changing their ways.

Society Max

Society Max is one of the crap shooters. He breaks a date with Mimi to play in Nathan's dice game.

Mimi

Mimi is a performer at the Hot Box. She dates the gambler Society Max and is angry with Nathan that Max has broken off a date to play craps.

Joey Perhaps

Joey Perhaps is one of the crap shooters.

Regret

Regret is one of the crap shooters.

Sky Rocket

Sky Rocket is one of the crap shooters.

Scranton Slim

Scranton Slim is one of the crap shooters.

Benny Southstreet

Benny Southstreet is a gambler and friend of Nathan's. Along with Nicely-Nicely Johnson, Benny attempts to help Nathan find a place for the crap game. He and Nicely lament the fact that Nathan gets distracted by Adelaide.

Themes

Love

Throughout *Guys and Dolls*, the notion of romantic love is often derided. Nathan repeatedly professes his love for Adelaide, but he has resisted marrying her for well over a decade. His friends regard him as caught, trapped by his relationship with her. Adelaide likewise views herself as caught, unable to break away from Nathan and find someone who might settle down and marry her because she is trapped by her love for him.

The musical number "Guys and Dolls," sung by Nicely and Benny in the first act, depicts love as something that compels men to behave in a way counter to their instincts. They cite a movie about a man who "sacrifices everything" for a woman. Discussing a story in the newspaper, they sing about a man who bought his wife a ruby with his union dues and about men who used to see a number of women and are now stuck watching television. Nicely and Benny describe the unique way men become "insane" when in love. A man who buys wine he cannot afford is likely doing it because he "is under the thumb of some little broad," they sing. In the lyrics to this song, the sentiment, expressed throughout the play as well, is conveyed that love makes men blind to the way women manipulate them. Love makes men helpless and women miserable.

Adelaide and Sarah both express angst, sadness, and frustration at loving men who disappoint them either through their behavior or character. Adelaide, in fact, is physically ill throughout the play seemingly because of her love for Nathan and his inability to follow through on promises to marry her. In song, Sky and Sarah describe the "helpless haze" they are in. Nathan similarly describes a feeling of helplessness. When Adelaide rages at him in the number "Sue Me," Nathan replies with a shrug, "Sue me, sue me, *What can you do me?* I love you *Give a holler and hate me, hate me,* Go ahead hate me / I love you." He seems genuinely baffled by his own feelings, knowing he loves Adelaide but not knowing how to change for her. At the play's end, he succumbs and agrees to marry her, but his sneeze suggests that he feels some reluctance. Love, as the play demonstrates, seems to require that Nathan change, and while he may be certain of his feelings, he doubts his ability to change. Sky, on the other hand, not only promises to change his ways but apparently follows up on his promises, as indicated by his membership in the Mission Band at the play's end.

Topics for Further Study

- *Guys and Dolls* is based on the short fiction of Damon Runyon. "The Idyll of Miss Sarah Brown" is the inspiration for the play's story line, but the play's writers were said to have also been inspired by other characters developed by Runyon, as well as by his style of dialogue. Read "The Idyll of Miss Sarah Brown" and compare it with *Guys and Dolls*. What elements appearing in the original were retained in the musical? What was changed, and what was left out? How successful were the musical writers in capturing the sounds of the characters' speech patterns as depicted by Runyon? Write a comparative essay in which you analyze these issues.

- As musical theater, *Guys and Dolls* integrates musical numbers within the play's narrative, often using a song to replace dialogue or to convey a character's private thoughts to the audience. Compose a scene into which you incorporate a short song sung between two characters or used to express one character's thoughts. Consider the ways in which the writers of *Guys and Dolls* created dialogue to introduce each song, thereby making them seem integrated with the play rather than simply added to the existing dialogue. Perform your scene for your classmates or record it and post to your Web page or YouTube. Invite classmates to review your production.

- In 1957, C. Y. Lee wrote the best-selling novel *Flower Drum Song*, which inspired the Rodgers and Hammerstein musical adaptation that premiered in 1958. In 1961, this story of a Chinese immigrant family was once again adapted, as the Rogers and Hammerstein musical was adapted for film. In 2002, Asian American playwright David Henry Hwang wrote a revival of the original musical for Broadway, attempting to make it more accessible for modern audiences. Read Lee's original novel and compare it with the 1961 film, which Hwang has stated inspired his own interpretation of Lee's novel. How are the Chinese characters presented in the novel and on film? In what ways does the film perpetrate stereotypes of Asian Americans? How accurately do you think the film represents Lee's original characterizations? How do you think the movie would be perceived today in terms of its depiction of Chinese immigrants? Write an essay in which you discuss your opinions of the book and movie, giving specific evidence from both, or create a visual presentation, either with PowerPoint or as a Web page accessible by your classmates, in which you present your comparison.

- Set in the 1950s, Cynthia Kadohata's young-adult, Newbery Award–winning novel *Kira-Kira*, published in 2006, portrays the experiences of a Japanese American family living in Georgia. In examining their struggles with poverty and racial injustice, Kadohata depicts an entirely different world than that portrayed in *Guys and Dolls*, which is set in the same time period. With a small group, read *Kira-Kira*. Consider the way Kadohata portrays the setting of Georgia in the 1950s. Is it vividly described, and does it play an essential role in the story? From which character's point of view is the story narrated? Does the author switch narrators during the course of the story? Are there characters in the story to whom you relate on some level? Give some thought to the way the author portrays the racism that the characters experience, and think about your responses as you read these sections of the story. Discuss these issues with the members of your group, or create an online blog in which you share your ideas and analyses with one another.

Transformation

The personal transformation that love apparently inspires or requires is referred to repeatedly in the play. It is indicated, for example, in the "Guys and Dolls" number that Nicely and Benny sing, as they describe the way love changes men. Despite the fact that Benny and Nicely regard Adelaide as problematic in that she distracts Nathan, Nathan nevertheless changes little about his behavior in order to please her. Nathan makes promises to Adelaide, and she expects him to change, but then he continues to gamble and to apologize to her. Benny's and Nicely's fears about the way love changes men are unfounded in Nathan's case, as he seems unable to change. The futility of personal transformation also appears to be underscored by the perpetually empty Save-a-Soul Mission. Despite Sarah's and Arvide's proselytizing, none of the sinners to whom they preach seem interested in repenting or changing their ways. When the gamblers do arrive, it is because of a dice game rather than a desire to transform. Yet Sky appears to be ready and able to transform himself for Sarah. At the play's conclusion, after his marriage to Sarah, he is dressed as a missionary and now preaches to anyone who will listen about the dangers of sin.

Sarah and Adelaide come to the conclusion that the personal transformations they had hoped for in Sky and Nathan are not possible. Having believed that Sky and Nathan should and would change because they love Sarah and Adelaide, the women transform their attitudes and determine that they can induce changes in their men after they have married them. They still believe that they can compel others to change rather than accept the notion that personal transformation arises out of a desire to behave differently. Nathan's sneeze at the play's conclusion suggests that he still doubts his ability to be the man Adelaide wants him to be.

Style

Musical Theater

As a work of musical theater, *Guys and Dolls* incorporates song and dance into the fabric of the play's narrative. The musical numbers serve as a way for the characters to express feelings, and the lyrics often stand in for spoken dialogue. There are three types of musical numbers in *Guys and Dolls*. Some numbers are songs that the characters are actually performing for one another, as when the Mission Band sings "Follow the Fold" or when Adelaide and the Hot Box Girls perform "Bushel and a Peck" and "Take Back Your Mink." Other songs represent dialogue among a number of characters. "Fugue for Tin Horns," for example, sung by Benny, Nicely, and Rusty Charley, includes comments about the horse upon which the characters are betting; the song also serves as a means of introducing the play's focus on gambling. Similarly, "The Oldest Established" is performed by the gamblers in the play as they discuss Nathan Detroit's reputation for hosting crap games. Other numbers are more intimate and are sung between two characters expressing feelings for one another, as when Sky and Sarah sing "I've Never Been in Love Before." Adelaide additionally sings two solos, "Adelaide's Lament" and a reprise of this number in the second act. In these songs, Adelaide sings as a way of expressing private feelings of sadness and frustration with Nathan.

Romantic Comedy

Guys and Dolls is written in the style of a romantic comedy. It lightly and humorously treats the romances of Nathan and Adelaide, who are perpetually engaged, and of Sarah and Sky, who as a missionary and a gambler form an unlikely couple. The two romances are approached quite differently. Nathan and Adelaide entertain the audience through Adelaide's silly, naive nature and Nathan's fumbling excuses. After Nathan sends a message to Adelaide about not being able to elope because his aunt in Pittsburgh has come down with a tropical disease, Adelaide gives Sky a nonsensical message for Nathan: "Tell him I never want to talk to him again and have him phone me here."

The playwrights structured the play's romance between Sky and Sarah in such a way as to generate both comedy and conflict. Nathan bets Sky that he cannot get Sarah to go to Havana with him. She eventually does so, and the two begin to fall in love, so much so that Sarah is not even angry with Sky when he reveals that Nathan's bet was the only reason he approached her. Later, however, Sarah determines that as a "Mission doll," she cannot be involved with a gambler. She then tells Arvide rather angrily that Sky came to the mission not seeking salvation, but seeking her, seeming now to feel uneasy at having been sought out in this manner. After the quick resolution of their differences, Sarah and Sky marry. His complete reversal from gambler to missionary serves as another comic element in their unlikely romance.

Similarly, Nathan stops stalling and agrees to marry Adelaide, but his sneeze at the play's conclusion reminds the audience of Adelaide's cold, which she believed was caused by being strung along by Nathan for so long. Nathan seems to be developing a similar ailment, now that he is about to wed. The play's use of lighthearted, upbeat musical numbers, along with jokes about the way love makes men behave as though they are insane, contribute to the comedic elements of the story line.

Historical Context

1950s Broadway Musicals

During the 1950s, the Broadway musical as a genre enjoyed enormous popularity. As a genre, the musical play was born in the 1940s, beginning with the 1943 production of *Oklahoma!* written by composers Richard Rodgers and Oscar Hammerstein. The duo went on to write a number of other musicals in the 1940s and 1950s. As Stacy Ellen Wolf observes in *Changed for Good: A Feminist History of the Broadway Musical*, "While in fact fewer musicals opened in the 1950s [than in other decades], more made a profit and more have continued to be performed in revivals and school and community productions." A dominant theme of the musicals of this time period is romance. Popular productions of the 1950s featuring romantic relationships included Swerling, Burrows, and Loesser's *Guys and Dolls* and Rodgers and Hammerstein's *The King and I, My Fair Lady, and The Sound of Music*. Such productions were enormously popular among critics and audiences and frequently were adapted for film productions. Not only did theatrical musical productions spawn film adaptations, but the sound-track albums topped the music charts as well and became an integral part of the American popular music scene.

As Ethan Mordden comments in *Coming Up*

Roses: The Broadway Musical in the 1950s, "The musical then was central to American culture." A popular form of entertainment, the Broadway musical accounted for fifteen of the fifty-one shows during the 1949–1950 season. In his book, Mordden traces the ways the musicals of this time period transformed the conventions of the genre as well as where they honored them. *Guys and Dolls*, Mordden observes, like the traditional musical, features two romantic couples, but in *Guys and Dolls* it is difficult to ascertain which couple—Sky and Sarah or Nathan and Adelaide—takes the primary role in the narrative. Some 1950s musicals, such as 1950's *Call Me Madam*, typically incorporated wry references to topical, contemporary themes. Mordden notes that *Guys and Dolls* resisted this trend and instead "holds to the boundaries of its timeless Runyonland."

Literature in the 1950s

Trends in fiction in the 1950s represented a move away from the experimental modes that thrived during the years between World War I (1914–1918) and World War II (1939–1945) and that continued to prevail in new forms in the postwar years. Writers such as Ernest Hemingway, who published *Across the River and Into the Trees* in 1950 and *The Old Man and the Sea* in 1952, and John Steinbeck, who published *East of Eden* in 1952, were popular; their approaches to literature were regarded as innovative and literary yet accessible. Martin Halliwell observes in *American*

Culture in the 1950s that the mass paperback market grew rapidly after World War II, and genre fiction, such as crime writing and murder mysteries, became popular. In the world of poetry, new experiments with form were taking place.

Compare & Contrast

- **1950s:** *Guys and Dolls* debuts on Broadway in 1950. The musical runs for 1,194 performances and wins five Tony Awards: Best Musical, Best Actor in a Musical, Best Featured Actress in a Musical, Best Director, and Best Choreography.

    Today: *Guys and Dolls* has been revived numerous times on Broadway, most recently in 2009. This production is much less well received than the original 1950 production. *New York Times* reviewer Ben Brantley describes the work as "paralyzed by self-consciousness." Although the play is nominated for a 2009 Tony Award for Best Revival, the play runs for only 113 performances.

- **1950s:** American cultural tastes are broad. Musicals featuring romantic, comedic story lines are popular on Broadway, as evidenced by the success of such plays as *Guys and*

Dolls and *My Fair Lady*. In fiction, genre works are popular, as mass-market paperback production increases in the postwar years. Mickey Spillane's crime novels, such as *My Gun Is Quick* (1950), are a part of this trend, as are feminine middlebrow novels designed to appeal to middle-class women, such as Margaret Kennedy's *The Feast* (1950). The combination of literary themes and accessible writing also broadens the appeal of such authors as Ernest Hemingway and John Steinbeck, while those of the literary movement known as the Beat movement experiment with form and language and explore themes of freedom and experience.

Today: Like the literature and culture of the 1950s, twenty-first-century drama, film, and literature offer a range of stylistic varieties. Popular films entertain audiences with romantic and alternatively comedic or dramatic story lines, while in fiction the lines between popular fiction and literary fiction blur. Acclaimed works of literary fiction, such as Muriel Barbery's *The Elegance of the Hedgehog* (2006), as well as novels that become mainstays of the book-club set, including Kathryn Stockett's *The Help* (2009), are adapted for the screen. The popularity of the musical is seen not only on Broadway, which routinely features a number of musicals (many of which are revivals of earlier productions), but on television as well, such as in the widely popular television series *Glee*, which centers on a high-school glee club.

- **1950s:** The world of illegal gambling comes under the scrutiny of the U.S. Senate via the Kefauver Committee, which is established in 1950 to investigate organized crime and which subsequently reveals the extent to which local officials are involved in illegal gambling and racketeering, among other crimes.

  Today: The world of gambling has expanded to include online gambling, some of which is legal and some of which is not. This realm has proved difficult to regulate. Additionally, since the 1950s, the U.S. government has expanded the category of legalized gaming, allowing regulated casino-type games and lotteries. There has also been an increase in the number of casinos operated by Native American tribes, to which different rules apply.

Poets such as Allen Ginsberg, Gary Snyder, Lawrence Ferlinghetti, Michael McClure, and Gregory Corso, among others, became known as the Beat poets, seeking new modes of poetic expression through experiments with sound, language, and form. Halliwell asserts, "This emphasis on poetic form was not a retreat into modernist experimentation, but the attempt to discover a new vocal range to speak to the rapidly transforming postwar nation." Such innovations and rejection of conventions stand in stark contrast to the Broadway musicals of the time period, which, though exploring new modes of marrying dramatic storytelling with musical numbers, presented society, culture, gender roles, and relationships in traditional, familiar ways.

New York Gambling in the 1950s

Ernest Havemann reported in *Life* magazine in June 1950 on the U.S. Senate's "full-scale probe of gambling and crime" that was then under way. According to Havemann, in the previous year, "about 50 million adult Americans as well as quite a number of minors" participated in "some form of gambling." Surveying the heavy losses suffered in the realm of legalized casino gambling, Havemann in his article also discusses gamblers from whom gambling racketeers profit and examines which types of gambling were most popular; these included betting on sporting events, in particular on horse racing. In exploring legal and illegal gambling, Havemann compares the fees and licenses paid by legal clubs to the bribes paid to officials by racketeers. Summarizing the activities and recommendations of the Kefauver Committee, named after the senator who headed the committee, Estes Kefauver of Tennessee, Havemann is critical of their efforts. He notes that senators investigating gambling and crime in the nation praised the city of New York for reducing the prevalence of bookmaking (betting) in the city. But Havemann insists that this reduction was due to the fact that the bribes demanded by the police were so high that the bookmakers took their business elsewhere, fleeing the city. The investigations of the Kefauver Committee were later applauded and have since been credited with revealing the extent to which organized crime families had infiltrated state and local governments at this time period in American history.

Critical Overview

Upon the 1950 Broadway debut of *Guys and Dolls*, *New York Times* critic Brooks Atkinson commented, "With a well-written book by Jo Swerling and Abe Burrows, and a dynamic score by Frank Loesser, it is a more coherent show than some that have higher artistic pretensions." Atkinson praises the play's "form, style and spirit," describing it as "gusty and uproarious" and stating that "it is not too grand to take a friendly, personal interest in the desperate affairs of Broadway's backroom society." In the *Dictionary of Literary Biography* volume *American Song Lyricists, 1920–1960*, Michael Lasser discusses the collaborative nature of the relationship between Burrows and Loesser. Lasser assesses Loesser's score, observing the ways in which it "combines comedy and skepticism, advances plot, and creates both atmosphere and character."

The nature of the creation of the playbook is sometimes a source of debate among theater critics. Caryl Brahms and Ned Sherrin, in an essay on Loesser for *The Guys and Dolls Book*, assert (as does Lasser) that Swerling's contribution to the play was minimal compared with that of Burrows. In their words, Loesser was "teamed with Abe Burrows (after an abortive book by Jo Swerling)." Yet Swerling's name is typically listed along with Burrows as writer, without any caveats or reservations. Swerling's son, Jo Swerling, Jr., defended his father in a 1992 letter to the editor in the *New York Times*. The junior Swerling insisted that "the book was written, the money was raised, and the show was cast and in rehearsal with the director before Burrows started on the project. He was brought in ... to snap up the dialogue." Yet Geoffrey Block, in *Enchanted Evenings: The Broadway Musical from "Show Boat" to Sondheim*, concurs that Swerling's work was minimal compared to that of Burrows. Block first describes the way the play's producers "commissioned Hollywood script writer Jo Swerling to write the book, and Loesser wrote as many as fourteen songs to match." Block then indicates that the producers and director George S. Kaufman were unhappy with Swerling's draft, as it "failed to match their vision of Runyonesque comedy. Burrows was then asked to come up with a new book to support Loesser's songs." Richard Hornby, in *Mad about Theatre*, emphasizes not the perceived rift between Swerling and the rest of the production but also the role of Kaufman in the development of the story in *Guys and Dolls*. Hornby asserts that in the play, "Swerling, Burrows and Kaufman flesh out the story in impressive ways."

What Do I Read Next?

- *Jelly's Last Jam* is an example of musical theater written and performed by African Americans. Based on the life of jazz musician Jelly Roll Morton, the play premiered in 1991 and was published in 1993. The playbook was written by George C. Wolfe and the lyrics by Susan Birkenhead, while the production utilized Morton's music for the score.

- The Rodgers and Hammerstein musical *The King and I*, which premiered and was published in 1951, features an Asian setting, as an English governess travels to Siam (now Thailand), where she is employed to instruct the king's offspring. Produced during the same period as *Guys and Dolls*, the musical adheres to the same theatrical and plot conventions and presents Siamese society from the point of view of English speakers.

- Like *Guys and Dolls*, *Bat 6*, a young-adult novel by Virginia Euwer Wolff, published in 2000, takes place shortly after World War II. Wolff's novel is set in Oregon and concerns the relationships of young teens preparing for a series of baseball games among rival towns. Two of the girls have been affected by the war more than the others; one lost her father in the Japanese attack on Pearl Harbor, and the other spent much of the war in a Japanese internment camp.

- *Broadway: The American Musical*, by Michael Kantor and Laurence Maslon, published in 2004, explores the history of the musical genre and serves as a companion resource to a Public Broadcasting System television series on the same subject.

- Mary Rose Wood's young-adult novel *My Life: The Musical*, published in 2008, uses musical theater as a basis for portraying not only friendships among teens but also the rich interior world they inhabit.

- Abe Burrows's memoir, *Honest, Abe: Is There No Business Like Show Business?* (1980), recounts the details of his career as a writer and includes his recollections about the creation of the playbook for Guys and Dolls.

- *Where's Charley?* is a musical by George Abbott and Frank Loesser, produced in 1948. The work represented Loesser's Broadway debut and established his reputation as a songwriter.

- Vaikom Mohammad Basheer's novella *Me Grandad 'ad an Elephant*, originally published in 1980, was produced as a musical play in 2011. The story focuses on a young Muslim-Malayali girl and her coming-of-age in a village in North Malabar.

Sources

Atkinson, Brooks, Review of *Guys and Dolls*, in *New York Times*, November 25, 1950.

Banner, Lisa, "Feminism," in *The Concise Princeton Encyclopedia of American Political History*, edited by Michael Kazin, Rebecca Edwards, and Adam Rothman, Princeton University Press, 2011, pp. 233–36.

Block, Geoffrey, *Enchanted Evenings: The Broadway Musical from "Show Boat" to Sondheim*, Oxford University Press, 1997, pp. 197–224.

Brahms, Caryl, and Ned Sherrin, "Frank Loesser," in *The Guys and Dolls Book*, Methuen, 1982, pp. 21–33.

Brantley, Ben, "It's a Cinch That the Bum Is Under the Thumb of Some Little Broad," in *New York Times*, March 2, 2009.

"Burrows, Abe," in *The Oxford Companion to American Theatre*, edited by Gerald Martin Bordman and Thomas S. Hischak, Oxford University Press, 2004, p. 102.

Carlan, Philip, Lisa Nored, and Ragan A. Downey, *An Introduction to Criminal Law*, Jones and Bartlett, 2011, p. 112.

Friedman, John S., "Introduction to the Kefauver Committee Report," in *The Secret Histories: Hidden Truths That Challenged the Past and*

Changed the World, edited by John S. Friedman, Picador, 2005, pp. 151–52.

"*Guys and Dolls* Revival to Close on Broadway June 14," in Broadway.com, June 10, 2009, http://www.broadway.com/buzz/99654/guys-and-dolls-revival-to-close-on-broadway-june-14/ (accessed August 28, 2011).

Halliwell, Martin, *American Culture in the 1950s*, Edinburgh University Press, 2007, pp. 51–84.

Havemann, Ernest, "Gambling in the U.S.," in *Life*, Vol. 28, No. 25, June 19, 1950, pp. 96, 108–109, 112–19, 121.

Hornby, Richard, *Mad about Theatre*, Applause, 1996, pp. 187–93.

Lasser, Michael, "Frank Loesser," in *Dictionary of Literary Biography*, Vol. 265, *American Song Lyricists, 1920–1960*, edited by Philip Furia, The Gale Group, 2002, pp. 336–53.

Loesser, Frank, Jo Swerling, and Abe Burrows, *Guys and Dolls*, in *The Guys and Dolls Book*, Methuen, 1982, pp. 44–124.

Mordden, Ethan, *Coming Up Roses: The Broadway Musical in the 1950s*, Oxford University Press, 1998, pp. 3–27, 28–36.

Naden, Corinne J., *The Golden Age of American Musical Theatre: 1943–1965*, Scarecrow Press, 2011, pp. 80–81.

Slater, Thomas, "Jo Swerling," in *Dictionary of Literary Biography*, Vol. 44, *American*

Screenwriters, Second Series, edited by Randall Clark, Gale Research, 1986, pp. 363–69.

Swerling, Jo, Jr., "*Guys and Dolls*; Abe Burrows: Undue Credit?" Letter to the Editor, in *New York Times*, May 3, 1992.

Wolf, Stacy Ellen, *Changed for Good: A Feminist History of the Broadway Musical*, Oxford University Press, 2011, pp. 25–52.

Further Reading

Barlow, Judith E., ed., *Plays by American Women: 1930–1960*, Applause Books, 2001.

> Barlow's collection gathers the work of prominent female American dramatists of the mid-twentieth century. In her introduction, Barlow discusses the influences of these women on contemporary American theater.

Breslin, Jimmy, *Damon Runyon: A Life*, Houghton Mifflin, 1991.

> Breslin's biography of Damon Runyon explores his career as a journalist and short-story writer and discusses the way Runyon came to be associated with New York's Broadway scene.

Durham, Steve, and Kathryn Hashimoto, *The History of Gambling in America*, Prentice Hall, 2009.

> Durham and Hashimoto's volume offers an assessment of gambling in the United States, discussing gaming among European settlers and the role of organized crime in developing the gambling industry in modern America.

Kenrick, John, *Musical Theatre: A History*, Continuum, 2008.

> Kenrick's history of musical theater explores the ancient predecessors of the genre in Greece and Rome and arrives at the modern American Broadway musical, also discussing the way musical theater evolved in other countries throughout the centuries.

Loesser, Susan, *A Most Remarkable Fella: Frank Loesser and the Guys and Dolls in His Life; A Portrait by His Daughter*, Donald I. Fine, 1993.

> This book, by Loesser's daughter, functions as both biography of Loesser and as her personal memoir about her father and her childhood. The work includes Susan Loesser's account of the controversy surrounding Jo Swerling's role in the writing of the *Guys and Dolls* playbook.

Runyon, Damon, *Guys and Dolls: The Stories of Damon Runyon*, Penguin, 1992.

> This collection of Runyon's short fiction includes the pieces that inspired the creators of the musical *Guys and Dolls*. William Kennedy offers an introduction to Runyon's stories.

Suggested Search Terms

Swerling, Burrows, Loesser AND Guys and Dolls
Guys and Dolls AND Broadway AND 1950

Guys and Dolls AND Broadway AND 1992

Guys and Dolls AND Broadway AND 2009

Loesser AND Guys and Dolls AND musical theater Loesser AND Guys and Dolls AND film Guys and Dolls AND 1950 AND gender roles Guys and Dolls AND 1950 AND gambling Guys and Dolls AND 1950 AND romantic comedy Guys and Dolls AND Burrows AND Swerling AND authorship